MOTHER
of
the
AMERICAS

MOTHER
of
the
AMERICAS

By Robert Feeney

Second edition, completely revised

AQUINAS
PRESS

IMPRIMATUR:　　✠ Thomas J. Welsh
　　　　　　　　　 Bishop of Allentown
　　　　　　　　　 Feast of Our Lady of Guadalupe
　　　　　　　　　 December 12, 1992

Cover Photo by Frank Smoczynski

Dedicated to Pope John Paul II, Mary's strong and humble servant; to my wife, Catherine, and daughter, Mary Ann; and to my mother, Mary Ellen, and in memory of my father, Bill.

Acknowledgments

Special appreciation to Archbishop Edward A. McCarthy for his Foreword; also to those who gave their endorsements: Cardinal Anthony Bevilacqua, Bishop Sean O'Malley, O.F.M. Cap., Bishop Thomas J. Welsh and Bishop John J. Meyers.

Thanks to Frank Smoczynski for the cover photo and other illustrations, also to Franciscan Marytown Press for their permission to quote from, *Handbook on Guadalupe;* also, to Ave Maria Institute in permitting me to use their fine book, *Am I Not Here.*

Thanks also to Fr. Christopher Rengers, O.F.M.Cap., for permission to quote from his excellent article on the infra-red studies of Mary's image; also, to Dr. Carson Daly for commenting on the manuscript and to Daniel Engler for proofreading it.

Special gratitude to my wife, Catherine, for her assistance and encouragement, and to my little daughter, Mary Ann, for her prayers.

Contents

Prefatory Notes

DEVOTION TO OUR BLESSED MOTHER should be at the heart of the prayer of every Catholic. This book, *Mother of the Americas*, promotes this devotion by explaining the apparition of Our Lady of Guadalupe and offering insights into this special event by the Popes of our times. Reading this work should definitely help to foster one's faith in the Lord Jesus and in Mary, His Blessed Mother.

✠ Anthony Cardinal Bevilacqua
Archbishop of Philadelphia

A Millennium of Hope is what Pope John Paul is calling us to look for as we face a new century.

Our temptation may be to wonder is it possible. Abortion, pornography, divorce, plus the national debt and the jobless rate; add in Somalia and Bosnia: does this add up to a millennium of hope?

Before you answer, read this little book of Bob Feeney's. Our Lady of Guadalupe, Mother of the Americas, Star of Evangelization do spell HOPE.

A warning: the Holy Father says the Church exists to evangelize. This book will help you say "I must evangelize too."

✠ Thomas J. Welsh
Bishop of Allentown

Mother of the Americas is truly a labor of love undertaken by a veteran Marian Apostle. The end result is an attractive and informative book graced with many photos and illustrations. I would not hesitate to endorse this most valuable work to my people.

✠ Sean O'Malley, O.F.M. Cap.
Bishop of Fall River

I find *Mother of the Americas* to be a very helpful book. It brings together in one volume much information about Our Blessed Mother's appearances to Juan Diego and the impact of those appearances on the life of the Church in Mexico and throughout the Americas. The book captures something of the simple faith and reverence of Juan Diego. It is an invitation to all of us to grow in our devotion to the Blessed Virgin Mary.

✠ John J. Meyers
Bishop of Peoria

Foreword

OUR BELOVED HOLY FATHER has frequently proclaimed to members of the Church in our day the challenge to evangelize, to transform our world by living and proclaiming the gospel of Jesus Christ.

On the occasion when Pope John Paul II called for the year 1992, the V Centenary of the coming of the Gospel to our hemisphere, to be a year of evangelization with a new fervor, the Pope said: "With the power of the cross ... with the torch of Christ in your hands and full of love for man, go forth, Church of the new evangelization. Thus you will be able to create a new dawn for the Church. And we shall all glorify the Lord of truth with the prayer which Columbus' seamen recited at dawn: 'Blessed be the light and the holy true cross and the Lord of Truth and the Holy Trinity ...'" (Address in Santo Domingo, October 12, 1984.)

Pope Paul VI, in his classic exhortation on evangelization (*On Evangelization in the Modern World*, December 8, 1975), spoke of the role of Mary, our mother, in evangelization: ..."This is the desire," he said, "that we rejoice to entrust to the hands and the heart of the Immaculate Blessed Virgin Mary ... On the morning of Pentecost she watched over with her prayer the beginning of evangelization prompted by the Holy Spirit: may she be the star of the evangelization ever renewed which the Church, docile to Our Lord's command, must promote and accomplish, especially in these times which are difficult but full of hope!"

This little volume, *Mother of the Americas*, by Robert Feeney, is enriched by a great number of utterances of the Popes and quotations of other authentic documents that enlighten our minds and warm our hearts as we reflect on the special role of Our Lady, the Mother of God, in living and proclaming the good news of her son Jesus Christ.

May readers of *Mother of the Americas* find inspiration to respond to the Bishops of the United States when they said, "We entrust our observance of the Quincentennial Year, our commitment to giving birth with new fervor to the life of the Gospel in our hemisphere, to Our Lady of Guadalupe, Patroness of the Americas. She truly was the first Christ bearer; by her maternal intercession, may her faithful sons and daughters be renewed and discover afresh the joy and splendor and promise of being bearers of Good News." (*Heritage and Hope, Evangelization in the United States,* November 1990.)

✠ Edward A. McCarthy
Archbishop of Miami

Introduction

WE CAN TRULY SAY that America is the land of Mary. This does not mean just the United States, but all of America — the entire Western Hemisphere. Every piece of land has been dedicated to her. This dedication of America took place in Mexico City in December of 1531, at a time when there were no national boundaries — it was just the New World. Mary dedicated America to herself in her talks with Juan Diego when she specifically claimed him and "all the people of these lands and all who come to me" as her children.

Mexico City, almost exactly the mid-point of the north and south continents of America, was the only capital city then known in the Americas. Mary claimed all these lands for herself. Therefore, we hail her as the Mother of the Americas and as Queen of the Americas. Those who refer to Holy Mary of Guadalupe as "the Mexican Virgin" are only aware of part of the truth, for she is really, as Pope Pius XII said, Empress of the Americas. The year that the Pope addressed her with this title, 1945, was the 50th anniversary of the coronation of the image of Our Lady of Guadalupe. The Holy Father noted that she had been Queen of all these lands from the moment of her apparitions in 1531. The following words are excerpted from his radio address to those gathered for the Guadalupe coronation ceremonies at the Basilica on October 12, 1945:

Hail, Fount most abundant from which springs the streams of Divine Wisdom, repelling with the most pure and limpid waters of orthodoxy the turbulent waves of error. Hail, O Virgin of Guadalupe! We to whom the admirable ordering of divine Providence has confided—without taking into consideration our unworthiness—the sacred treasure of Divine Wisdom on earth, for the salvation of all souls, place again above your brow the crown, which puts forever under your powerful patronage the purity and integrity of the holy faith in Mexico and in all the American continent. We are certain that while you are recognized as Queen and Mother, America and Mexico will be saved.

Pope John XXIII also prayed to her as Mother of the Americas and Heavenly Missionary of the New World (October 12, 1961). He addressed her as Mother and Teacher of the Faith to the peoples of the Americas. He prayed that, favored by her benign care, Catholic education, in the shelter of the home, might achieve wholesome growth.

On January 27, 1979, Pope John Paul II, the first pope to visit the Basilica of Our Lady of Guadalupe, called for evangelization, invoking the faith of Mary as a model for the faith of all Christians. He called her the "Star of Evangelization," knelt before her image, invoked her motherly assistance, and called upon her as Mother of the Americas.

On May 6, 1990, the Holy Father returned to the Basilica in Mexico City and again looked to Mary to continue to be the "Star of the New Evangelization." The Pope, upon his arrival in Mexico City, spoke of Our Lady of Guadalupe as being "the first to evangelize America."

In a message to the President of the U.S. National Conference of Catholic Bishops, dated October 28, 1991, Pope John Paul II stated that he is praying that Our Lady of Guadalupe will watch over the people of the United

States as they seek to respond to the new challenges of the present time, now that we are at the threshold of the Third Christian Millennium.

The Holy Father called for us to observe 1992 as a 500th Anniversary Year of Evangelization in the New World. He called for this celebration to be the dawn of a "new evangelization: new in its ardor, its methods, its expression." He is encouraging everyone in the Americas to participate in the "New Evangelization." The U.S. Bishops have entrusted this Fifth Centenary observance to Our Lady of Guadalupe, Patroness of the Americas.

The Pope made a visit to Santo Domingo, Dominican Republic from October 9-14, 1992, to honor the 500th Anniversary of the Evangelization of America. During his visit there, he spoke of Mary's role in the first evangelization of America and invoked her guidance in its new evangelization. During the celebration of the Mass on October 12, 1992, he recited an Act of Entrustment, consecrating to Mary, the present and past of the Americas.

It is my hope that people will join themselves in prayer, with Mary, preparing their hearts to receive the Holy Spirit in order to be transformed by His gifts. May the Holy Spirit help us prepare for the year 2000 and, through Mary, renew the face of the earth.

Robert Feeney

Cardinal Jozef Tomko, Prefect of the Congregation for the Evangelization of Peoples, kneels at the site where Columbus landed on San Salvador and planted the cross of Christ.

1

The Arrival of Catholicism

DUE TO THE DISCOVERY of America by Christopher Columbus, the peoples of the New World were able to be opened up to the proclamation of the Gospel. Columbus, born in Genoa, Italy, in 1451, started out for America on August 3, 1492, from Palos, Spain, with the support of the Spanish monarchs, Ferdinand and Isabella. On the first voyage, three vessels carried a total of 120 men: the flagship, *Santa Maria,* the *Pinta*, and the *Nina*. Before leaving, Columbus and his men received the Sacraments of Penance and Holy Eucharist from Father Juan Perez. Columbus also took his men in procession to the monastery of LaRabida to put themselves under the special protection of the Mother of God. After he and his men left Palos on their journey, every evening they sang the Salve Regina and the Ave Maris Stella aboard their ships. At 2 A.M. on October 12th, one of the *Pinto's* crew sighted land, and in the forenoon, Columbus landed on an island. He named the island, San Salvador, in honor of Our Savior and planted the cross of Christ there. He then discovered the island of La Espanola and established the first Spanish settlement in the New World before returning to Spain.

Evangelization began with the second voyage of Columbus, who was accompanied by the first missionaries. The sowing of the gift of faith began with their arrival. On January 6, 1494, on the island of La Espanola (today the Domincan Republic and Haiti), the first Mass in the New World was celebrated by Father Bernardo Boyl, designated Vicar Apostolic of the New World, in the presence of twelve other priests and religious.

Ramon Pane, a religious of the Order of St. Jerome, together with Franciscans Juan de Duelle and Juan de Tissin, were the first to evangelize the inhabitants of this land. On September 21, 1496, Guaticagua, the local chief, became the first person to be baptized in the New World.

On August 6, 1511, Pope Julius II created the Dioceses of Santo Domingo, La Vega and Puerto Rico, the first in the New World. Bishop Pedro Suarez of La Vega was the first Bishop to arrive in the New World.

The Domincans arrived in Santo Domingo in 1510. Back in Spain, Domincan Francisco de Victoria lectured at the University of Salamanca on the dignity of the Indians. He articulated a genuine code of human rights. This was an effort of his to direct the work of the colonization in the New World. In 1511, Dominican Anton Montesinos preached in Santo Domingo about respect for the human rights of the Indians. The Domincan superior, Pedro de Cordova, recorded all that Fr. Montesinos taught and compiled this into America's first catechism. The Dominicans founded a studium generale that Pope Paul III, in 1538, raised to the status of a university, the first in America.

In 1514, the first Marian shrine in the New World was established in the city of Higuey. There Our Lady of Altagracia was venerated and is the first known place of Marian devotion to be built on American soil.

Hernando Cortez was born in the province of Extremadra in Spain in 1485. Cortez set sail in 1504 for La Espanola to seek his fortune. He remained there until 1511, when he joined with Diego Velasquez to conquer Cuba. Cortez became the first mayor of Santiago de Cuba, and Velasquez, the Governor of Cuba, was given powers of exploration. Velasquez sent Cortez on an expedition in 1519 to the Yucatan area in Mexico. Cortez took with him 600 men and soon founded the town of Veracruz. Cortez, when met by the Indians of that area, quickly sensed the political climate of the new land:

> He had a genius for understanding the entire scope of any given situation, and the situation in Mexico at the time of his arrival was basically very simple, although it might have appeared highly complex to a less perceptive leader. Through interpreters, Cortez learned that all of the smaller Indian nations were ruled by the Aztec Emperor, Montezuma, whose grandfather had built an empire on their tribute of gold, food, and human lives. It took a man like Cortez only a matter of days to perceive and play upon the fact that these smaller nations, like enslaved people in any era or clime, hated the tyrant and lacked only a strong leader to unite them against his rule. They were eager to put an end to decades of heavy taxation and bloody tribute, the latter being paid annually in the form of human victims for the great Aztec Festive Days, when as many as 25,000 human sacrifices were offered up to the gods in a single year.[1]

Toward the middle of August 1519, Cortez started toward Mexico City. The Spaniards were appalled at what they encountered along the way: hideous bloodstained idols of the Indian gods. Cortez ordered that the temples be cleansed and the images be cast down and replaced with crucifixes and statues of the Madonna on the altars atop the pyramids. When Cortez entered Mexico City, he placed Montezuma under house arrest and held him as a hostage. The Spanish leader told Montezuma about the Mother of

God and through her intercession tried to convert him to the Catholic faith and to abandon his gods. Montezuma seemed unmoved, and Cortez spoke out against the pagan gods. He even struck down the central image, Huilzilopochtli, cast it down the steps of the temple, and ordered the Madonna to be placed there. The Indians fought back and forced the Spaniards out of the city. Cortez, however, rallied Indians hostile to Montezuma, then with his band of men entered the city again — this time engaging in a fierce battle in August, 1521, which led to the complete conquest of Mexico. Cortez ordered that all the idols be destroyed and all pagan worship cease, but he could not evangelize the Indians because he had only one priest, the chaplain, Father Olmedo. Cortez wrote to Emperor Charles V of Spain and requested missionaries for the Aztec Empire.

The evangelization of Mexico began with the arrival in Mexico City of the first 12 Franciscans on June 18, 1524, sent by Pope Adrian VI. The Dominicans came in 1526. The missionaries devoted themselves tirelessly to evangelization, though they faced slow progress in the early years. Among the first to be converted to the Catholic faith was an Indian named Cuauhlatohuac, meaning singing eagle, and his wife and uncle. After being baptized, Cuauhlatohuac took the name Juan Diego, his wife and uncle took the names Maria Lucia and Juan Bernardino.

2
The Apparitions

First Apparition

At dawn, on the morning of December 9, 1531, Juan
Diego, a middle-aged Indian recently converted to the
Catholic faith, was hurrying to attend the Mass of the
Blessed Virgin in the Franciscan Church of Tlaltelolco,
when something remarkable happened. When he heard
the sound of sweet music coming from the top of Tepeyac
Hill, a barren knoll about 130 feet high on the outskirts of
Mexico City, he stopped to listen to what he thought was
the sound of birds singing in harmony. Were these some
rare birds singing in the sky? While he was looking at the
spot where the music came from, he saw a brilliant cloud
which seemed to be getting brighter. "Suddenly he
became aware that the music had stopped, then he heard
the melodious voice of a young woman calling him:
'Juanito, dear Juan Dieguito.'"² He moved to follow the
voice that was speaking his name in the manner of a
mother calling a child. When he reached the top, he saw a
beautiful young maiden standing in front of the brilliant
cloud. As he approached her, his senses became so filled
with visual and auditory beauty and with spiritual joy
that all he could do was kneel and smile up at her. She
was surrounded by a glow of light which dimmed the sun,
a light which cast wonderful colors over the parched,

Juan Diego on his way to Mass on December 9, 1531, when suddenly he heard Mary's sweet voice calling him: "Juanito, dear Juan Dieguito."

rocky hill. The rocky cliff reflected the light or rainbow-colored stones, gleaming as from an inner fire. Her garments shone with the same strange light, but Juan Diego forgot the splendor of light and color when he looked at her face. He saw a young face with lovely eyes and a smile of loving compassion. She spoke in his native language, Nahuatl, saying, "Juanito, my little son whom I love tenderly like a little child, where are you going?" Juan Diego replied: "My Lady, I am on my way to the church in Tlaltelolco to attend Mass and to study and learn the divine mysteries that the priests teach us."

She replied:

> Know for certain, littlest of my sons, that I am the perfect and perpetual Virgin Mary, Mother of the true God through Whom everything lives, the Lord of all things near and far, the Master of Heaven and Earth. I wish and intensely desire that in this place my sanctuary be erected. Here I will demonstrate, I will exhibit, I will give all my love, my compassion, my help and my protection to the people. I am your merciful mother. The merciful mother of all of you who live united in this land, and of all mankind, of all those who love me, of those who cry to me, those who seek me, of those who have confidence in me. Here I will hear their weeping, their sorrow, and will remedy and alleviate all their multiple sufferings, necessities and misfortunes. In order that my wish may be fulfilled, you must go to Mexico City, to the house of the Bishop and tell him that I sent you, that it is my desire to have a sanctuary built for me here. Tell him what you have seen and heard and be sure that I shall be grateful to you for doing what I ask. I shall make you happy and reward you for the service which you render to me. My son, you have heard my wish. Go in peace.

Juan showed unquestioning obedience as Mary herself had in her own divine mission. He hurried down the hill into the city and knocked on the gate of Franciscan Bishop-elect Juan Zumarraga (not consecrated Bishop yet, but exercising episcopal jurisdiction). The servants viewed Juan Diego as an unwelcome visitor and only with much difficulty was he allowed to see the Bishop. Zumarraga withheld judgment, told Juan that he would ponder what he had said, and instructed him to come back in a few days. Crestfallen, Juan went back to see Mary. He did not know how to explain to her his seeming lack of success.[3]

Second Apparition

Later in the afternoon of the same day, Juan returned to the hill and found Mary waiting to hear about the success of his mission. He ran to her and knelt, flooded with a peace that erased his fears. He said, "My beautiful Lady, My Queen, My Love! I gave your message to the Lord Bishop but he did not believe me. So I beg you to send a person of high and noble rank who will merit respect, someone well-known and esteemed in order that he may be believed." The Lady looked on him with compassion and said, "Hear me, my beloved son, and understand that I have many servants who would willingly carry out my wish, but it is necessary that through your intervention my desire shall be fulfilled. I ask you, my son, to go again to the Bishop and to repeat what you have told him before." Juan felt his courage returning. The next day, December 10, Juan Diego went to Tlaltelolco to assist at Holy Mass. Afterward, he went to the Bishop's residence. Bursting into tears, he said that he had talked to the Mother of God a second time and that she had sent him to ask that a sanctuary be built for her at the foot of Tepeyac Hill.

This time the Bishop was impressed with Juan's humble sincerity and listened to him attentively. The Bishop, who felt inclined to believe him, said, "My son, I am interested in what you have to say. Perhaps you could bring me some sign or proof from the Lady in order to be convinced that she definitely wants a sanctuary built at Tepeyac." Juan,

Juan Diego humbly and attentively listening to Mary tell him who she is and what his mission is going to be.

Juan Diego telling the Bishop-elect Our Lady's desire to have a sanctuary built for her.

having great faith that Mary would give him a sign, agreed to bring one back to him. The Bishop was pleased with his attitude.

Third Apparition

Later that same day, Juan arrived back at the hill of Tepeyac and found Mary there. Juan told Mary that the Bishop wanted a sign in order to assure him that the message really came from her. The Blessed Virgin listened to him and reassuringly said:

> So be it, my son. Come back tomorrow morning and I will give you the sign which will assure him and he will no longer doubt you. Be sure, my son, that you will be compensated for all the trouble, work and fatigue that you have suffered for me; go in peace, tomorrow I shall be waiting for you here.

When Juan reached his home, the town of Tolpetlac, that evening, he found his uncle, Juan Bernardino, very sick with a fever. Distressed by his uncle's condition, he spent the next day, Monday, nursing him, and was therefore unable to keep his appointment with the Lady at Tepeyac. In spite of Juan's loving care and the medicines he administered, his uncle grew worse. Fearing that his uncle might die, Juan on the next day, December 12, left the town of Tolpetlac and started on his way to the Franciscan church at Tlaltelolco, St. James, to bring a priest to administer the last sacraments to his dying uncle.

Fourth Apparition

As Juan approached Tepeyac Hill, he suddenly remembered that he had forgotten to keep his appointment with the Virgin Mary. Perhaps, he reasoned, the Lady might not see him and detain him if he took the road on the east side of Tepeyac Hill. To his surprise he saw her coming down from the hill, and going out on the east road, awaiting his approach. He was overwhelmed with sadness for having disappointed her and he bowed down to greet her, wishing her good-day. Juan explained his mission for his uncle. He said to her, "After I succeed in doing this duty, I will return to you and deliver your message, please be patient with me for the moment." As he spoke, she smiled at him and regarded him with loving compassion. She replied:

> Hear and let it penetrate into your heart, my dear little son: let nothing discourage you, nothing depress you; let nothing alter your heart or your countenance. Also do not fear any illness or vexation, anxiety or pain. Am I not here who am your Mother? Are you not under my shadow and protection? Am I not your fountain of life? Are you not in the folds of my mantle, in the crossing of my arms? Is there anything else that you need? As for your uncle's illness, it is not unto death. At this moment I ask you to believe that he is already cured.

Juan heard these consoling words spoken by Mary and was relieved of his concern for his uncle. She instructed him to climb to the top of the hill where he had first seen her. She said that he would find many flowers blooming there, but that he should bring only the roses to her. Juan knew that flowers never bloomed in that place, but since he trusted her, he went to the top of the hill. There he found and gathered beautiful Castilian roses covered with dew and filling the morning air with heavenly perfume. Gathering together the ends of his cloak, or tilma, he carried the roses that he had cut and presented them to Mary. She took the roses into her immaculate hands, rearranged them in his cloak, and tied the ends of his cloak in a knot at the back of his neck. She said:

> This is the sign that you are to take to the Lord Bishop. Tell him in my name that in these roses he will see my will and accomplish it. Juan, you are my ambassador and worthy of my confidence. Do not let anyone see what you are carrying; do not unfold your cloak until you are in his presence. Tell him all that you have seen and heard, omitting nothing. Tell him that I sent you to the top of the hill to gather the flowers there. Repeat the

This statue marks the spot where Mary spoke to Juan Diego on December 12, 1531, as he was on his way to get a priest for his dying uncle.

Juan Diego gathered roses in December on top of Tepeyac Hill and Mary arranged them into his cloak to take back as a sign for the Bishop.

story completely so that the Bishop will believe you and will build the sanctuary for which I have pleaded.

Juan set out on his mission with a joyful heart. The Bishop's servants were rude, but Juan waited patiently for some time until they told the Bishop of his presence. Finally, Juan was permitted to see the Bishop. After greeting him, Juan gave him the Virgin Mary's message. As the Indian unfolded his cloak, roses spilled to the floor. They lay at his feet, still bright with dew and delicately fragrant; and suddenly the precious image of the Immaculate Virgin Mary, the Mother of the true God, appeared on his cloak, miraculously imprinted. All present fell on their knees, and the Bishop, with tears in his eyes, cried, "It is the Immaculate Virgin Mary!" He recited the Hail Mary before the image and implored the Blessed Virgin to pardon him for not having believed in the beginning. When the Bishop got up, he untied the cloak fastened around Juan's neck and reverently placed it in his private oratory. Tearfully the Bishop gave thanks to God and to Mary. The Bishop kept Juan in his home all day and on Wednesday the prelate and Juan walked to the places where Juan had seen and conversed with Mary. The Bishop then gave him permission to return to his uncle, who had nearly died the day before.

Fifth Apparition

Just after Juan Diego had left his uncle to fetch a priest, a lady of indescribable beauty appeared to his dying uncle in Tolpetlac. The room was flooded with a soft light and Mary had cured him, telling him that she wanted a sanctuary built at Tepeyac Hill. She asked him to go to the Bishop and inform him of the manner in which she had cured him and to tell him that she wished her image to be called "Holy Mary of Guadalupe." This all took place on December 12.

As Juan unfolded his cloak, roses fell to the floor and suddenly, the precious image of Mary appeared on his cloak.

Mary appears to Juan Bernardino in Tolpetlac and cures him. She wishes her image to be called "Holy Mary of Guadalupe."

3

The Miraculous Image of Mary

T HE BEAUTIFUL IMAGE of Mary on the cloak of Juan Diego is today venerated in the new Basilica of Our Lady of Guadalupe. Dedicated on October 12, 1976, the new church is located next to the old Basilica, at the bottom of Tepeyac Hill, four miles from central Mexico City.

The cloak, which was made by Juan's wife, Maria Lucia, consists of two pieces of fabric about six feet long and made from the fibers of the maguay plant. Experts say that anything made of the maguay plant should deteriorate within 20 years, but the image has remained intact more than 450 years! Painted with "brushes which were not of this earth," as Pope Pius XII declared, this charming image is as beautiful and fresh today as when it miraculously appeared on the cloak of Juan Diego in 1531.

Mary's image is life-size — four feet, eight inches tall. To many people who look at the image, she appears as a young Jewish maiden, with beautiful features, no older than 15. Dressed in what appears to be the garb of a Nazarean of 2,000 years ago, this image portrays, many people believe, Mary as the Child Jesus saw her, delight-

Pope Pius XII declared that this image is painted with "brushes not of this earth."

ing in her beauty, femininity, and motherliness. We can also see in Mary what Jesus saw: a woman of faith, strength, and obedience to God's Holy Will.

In the image, Mary's loving eyes show her compassion and love for us. Her eyes express her lowliness and her tenderness. If, as is often said, the eyes are the windows of the soul, in Mary's eyes we can see reflected the love and care which she showers upon us as she once did upon Jesus. Mary's eyes show forth her mercy as she invites all of us to come to her as trusting little children and to invoke her maternal aid. Her eyes invite us to trust her completely, and to be carried by her in complete self-abandonment.

Her folded hands show us the reverence, honor, and respect due to the Blessed Trinity. The prayerful position also reminds us that Mary continually intercedes for us with the Blessed Trinity and that God sends all His graces, virtues, and gifts to us through Mary's hands.

Although her heart is not pictured, this image inspires us to pray to Mary, and by our prayers to touch and move her maternal heart, where we all can meet. As Mary said to Juan Diego: "Are you not in the crossing of my arms?" Meditating on these words, we are drawn to place ourselves in the crossing of Mary's arms and to rest on her maternal heart.

The beautiful image of Mary is today venerated in the new Basilica, dedicated on October 12, 1976.

The miraculous image of Mary is seen in the Basilica behind the main altar.

President and Mrs. John F. Kennedy visited the Shrine and attended Mass at the old Basilica on July 2, 1962.

Mary's eyes show her compassion and love for us.
Pope John Paul II said: "I feel drawn to this picture of
Our Lady of Guadalupe because her face is full of kindness
and simplicity . . . it calls me."

4

The Personalities

Juan Diego

Juan Diego was born in Cuautitlan, about 14 miles away from Mexico City, in 1474, the year Isabella ascended the throne of Castile and 18 years before Columbus discovered America. He and all his friends were Aztecs. He was married to a woman named Maria Lucia, and both were baptized in 1525 by a Franciscan priest. He belonged to the large middle class of Aztecs, called the Mazehuales. He manufactured mats called "petates" and was very successful in his work. There was great demand at the time for mats: for merchants displaying their wares, for decorations, for bedding, for curtains on doors and windows, and for floor coverings. He was a full-fledged citizen, a landowner entitled to vote in elections. Very happily married to Maria Lucia, he farmed the land next to his house in Cuautitlan, growing corn, beans, and assorted vegetables. On occasion he also hunted deer and turkey for the family's meat. He and his wife cheerfully walked the 14 miles to Tlaltelolco to attend Mass on both Saturday and Sunday, and to receive religious instructions. In 1529, his wife, Maria, became sick and died. Juan suffered greatly with the loss of his wife, though he was consoled by intense devotion to Mary. Because he was so lonely, he moved to Tolpetlac, 9 miles from Mexico City, to live nearer to his uncle, Juan Bernardino. In this town, Juan built a house not far from his uncle on a large piece of property he had already owned. He regularly attended Mass on Saturday in honor of the Mother of God, and it was on one such Saturday, December 9, 1531, that Mary appeared to him. He was 57 years old that year. At that time the Feast of the Immaculate Conception was celebrated on December 9. "After the miracle of Guadalupe, Juan Diego moved to a room attached to the chapel that housed the sacred image of Our Lady of Guadalupe, after having given his business and property to his uncle."[4] He spent the last 17 years of his life propagating the account of his experiences with the Blessed Virgin. As a result of his efforts and of seeing the miraculous image of Mary, within seven years eight million Aztec Indians were converted to the Catholic faith. He explained to his countrymen the words of the Blessed Virgin and sent the new enthusiasts to the Franciscan missionaries to be instructed in the Catholic faith. He continued his custodianship of the sacred image, praying before the image, and continuing to counsel and teach his countrymen. The people who knew Juan Diego called him "the Pilgrim," because he always walked alone and always seemed contemplative." He served as a model of the saintly life until his death on May 30, 1548, at the age of 74. Caring for his dear Lady's image brought about a profound change in him that was obvious to his countrymen."[5] Juan Diego is a fine example for the laity. Through the grace of baptism, he was involved in the Church's mission of evangelization. His example reminds us what Pope John Paul II stresses: that lay involvement in the Church's mission is rooted in one's baptismal commitment and that through the awareness of the importance of baptism, all lay spirituality finds its authentic expressions. The Holy Father calls baptism "the sacrament of interior enlightenment and the basis of all Christian dignity, because it is the origin of incorporation into Christ." [6]

Juan Diego deeply loved the Holy Eucharist. By special permission of the Bishop, he received Holy Communion three times a week, a highly unusual occurrence in those days. His deep love for Our Lady of Guadalupe led him to a deep love for the Sacred Heart of Jesus in the Holy Eucharist. Juan Diego reminds us that true devotion to Mary leads us to her Son in the Holy Eucharist. She leads us to the Bread of Life, to Him Who said: "Come to me all you who labor and find life burdensome and I will refresh you." Mary leads us to Jesus Who said: "Learn from me, for I am gentle and lowly of heart."

Juan Diego has long been a subject of interest to his countrymen, who have traditionally esteemed his character. Since the apparitions of 1531, mothers have told their children, "May God treat you as He did Juan Diego!" We might also hope that Juan Diego will become a model and example for all lay apostles and for all people seeking to do the will of God through Holy Mary, His Mother.

In April of 1990, Juan Diego was declared Blessed by Pope John Paul II at the Vatican. The beatification ceremony was performed by the Pope on May 6, 1990, at the Basilica of Our Lady of Guadalupe in Mexico City. The Pope praised Juan Diego for his simple faith, nourished by catechesis; and pictured him as a model of humility. Pope John Paul II holds up Juan Diego as a model for the lay faithful, who are all called to share in the prophetic, priestly, and kingly role of Christ.

Juan de Zumarraga

Juan de Zumarraga, born in Spain in 1476, became a

Franciscan monk and by 1527 he was prior of the Monastery del Abrojo where Emperor Charles V went for a retreat during Holy Week. Upon leaving, he gave Friar Juan money for his community which Friar Juan distributed to the poor. When the Emperor heard of this he was pleased. Being convinced of the virtue of this saintly friar, he suggested to Pope Clement VII that he be given the bishopric of Mexico. Friar Juan arrived in the New World on December 6, 1528, and upon arrival decided to consecrate all the land of America to the Immaculate Virgin. The Bishop-elect experienced great difficulties as a result of the Indians' native religions and also because of their hatred for the Spaniards. He worried that the Indians and the Spaniards would destroy each other if they could. As a check on the civil authority, Charles V named Bishop Zumarraga "Protector of the Indians," which gave him added authority. The Bishop became increasingly aware that the situation between the Indians and the Spaniards could be saved by nothing less than a miracle.

Bishop Zumarraga, who was very devoted to Mary, begged her help and secretly asked for Castilian roses to be a manifestation of her response. The Bishop prayed long and hard: it does not seem accidental that when Juan Diego went to the Bishop and was asked for a sign, the sign that Mary sent was that of Castilian roses and her beautiful image on the cloak. This sign seems to have been a direct answer from heaven to the Bishop's secret prayers to Mary. It was through his love for Mary and his constant prayers that the sign of roses was granted.

The year after the Virgin's miraculous apparitions, Bishop-elect Zumarraga went to Spain to be consecrated Bishop. He spent two years there trying to obtain favors and privileges for the Indians. In 1548, he was appointed as the first Archbishop in the New World. He died in

Mexico City on June 3, 1548, at the age of 72. His remains are now in the crypt of the Metropolitan Cathedral. Archbishop Zumarraga's legacy was great: he was a leader, an active missionary, a great promoter of education, and a pious benefactor who, because of his kindness and charity to the poor, never accumulated earthly possessions. He established one of the first schools of higher learning in America, the College of the Holy Cross of Tlaltelolco, which went from primary up to the college level. He was responsible for the establishment of one of the first universities in America, the University of Mexico. He was also responsible for the first hospital in America. He brought the first printing press and printers to the New World from Europe. He also imported agricultural experts to show the Indians farming methods. Because he was very interested in improving the diet of the Mexicans, he imported new kinds of fruit trees.

Statue of Juan Diego on the site where he and his wife lived in Cuautitlan, located 14 miles outside of Mexico City.

Juan Diego and his wife weaving mats, which were their means of livelihood.

Church of St. James, located in Tlaltelolco, an area of Mexico City. Here Juan Diego and his wife were baptized and attended Holy Mass on Saturdays and Sundays.

Baptismal fount in the Church of St. James, where Juan and his wife were baptized.

5

The Merciful Motherhood of Mary

L ET US TAKE a closer look at Mary's loving words to Juan Diego and Juan Bernardino. As we have seen, she spoke to Juan Diego on the morning of December 9, saying: "Know for certain, least of my sons, that I am the perfect and perpetual Virgin Mary, Mother of the true God through Whom everything lives." In saying this, Mary confirmed the Church's traditional teaching that she is ever-Virgin. Mary's message teaches us of her divine maternity and inspires us to know that through the merits of her perfect and perpetual virginity, we will receive the gifts of grace which she promises.

Next, Mary asked for a special sanctuary to be built:

I wish and intensely desire that in this place my sanctuary be erected. Here I will demonstrate, I will exhibit, I will give all my love, my compassion, my help and my protection to the people. I am your merciful mother. The merciful mother of all of you who live united in this land, and of all mankind, of all those who love me, of those who cry to me, of those who seek me, of those who have confidence in me. Here I will hear their weeping, their sorrow, and will remedy, and alleviate all their multiple sufferings, necessities and misfortunes.

The late Monsignor Angel M. Garibay, cited in Helen Behrens' *The Virgin Mary of Guadalupe,* was one of the canons of the Basilica of Guadalupe and Professor of the Aztec language at the University of Mexico. He gives an enlightening interpretation of Mary's words to Juan Diego: Mary asks for, Mary promises, Mary affirms. With insistence she pleads for a sanctuary where she will show her love, compassion, help, and protection. With these four maternal activities she implicitly promises to be our mother and she explicitly declares, "I am your merciful mother." It is a solemn declaration of motherhood, as Mary, the Mother of Mercy.

When Mary appeared to Juan on his way to get a confessor for his uncle, she particularly promised peace of heart to those who would meditate on her message. *"Hear and let it penetrate into your heart, my dear little child: let nothing discourage you, nothing depress you. Let nothing alter your heart or your countenance. Also do not fear any illness or vexation, anxiety or pain."* She then says. *"Am I not here who am your mother? Are you not under my shadow and protection? Am I not your fountain of life? Are you not in the folds of my mantle, in the crossing of my arms? Is there anything else that you need?"* In asking these questions, Mary gives us reason for new courage and she demonstrates how close and constant her care is for us. Her questions encourage us. Mary tells us that we must fear nothing, that we are not alone in the world or without help. She reminds us that no evil is worthy of fear. She also tells us why our souls should be free of fear. "Am I not here? I am your mother. You are under my protection." She helps us understand that there will be illness, vexation, anxiety, and pain, but we are not to fear them, for we are under her protection.

The late Monsignor Garibay poetically describes Mary's maternal solicitude, comparing her to a tree with luxuriant foliage that protects from both the heat of the sun and cold of the rain, giving comfort and joy to whoever takes refuge under its branches. When Mary says, "I am your fountain of life," she promises not only the haven of a luxuriant tree, but also a river of grace. Her words offer well-being, contentment, and happiness. They affirm that Mary offers peace when she asks, "Are you not in the folds of my mantle, in the crossing of my arms?" Mary tells us that she protects and assists, that she gives peace, that she, with motherly tenderness, carries her children in her arms, presses them to her heart, and quiets and defends them.

6

Pope John Paul II and Guadalupe

T HE POPES DOWN through the centuries have favorably approved the apparitions of Our Lady of Guadalupe. Although the act of approbation was not given until 1754, indulgences were conferred by Pope Gregory XIII. Pope Innocent X, the first pontiff to receive a copy of the original image, put it in his personal room and venerated it.

Among all the popes, there was none who did as much to help the cause of the apparitions as did Pope Benedict XIV, who was pope from 1740-1758. When he saw the sacred image, he fell on his knees and exclaimed, "to no other nation has this been done." He then authorized the crowning of the image, but it was not officially crowned until 1895. Pope Pius VII ranked the sanctuary of Our Lady of Guadalupe second among Catholic churches, along with St. John Lateran in Rome.

In 1895, Pope Leo XIII had the image crowned in his name and he did many other things to spread devotion to Our Lady of Guadalupe. Pope Pius XII ordered the image to be crowned on October 12, 1945, the 50th anniversary of the coronation by Leo XIII. He pronounced her the Empress of all the Americas. Pope John XXIII composed

On January 27, 1979, Pope John Paul II was the first pope to visit the Shrine in Mexico City. He called upon Mary as "Mother of the Americas."

Pope John Paul II offered Holy Mass before the thousands of people who gathered in the Basilica. He urged Catholics to stress evangelization and he entrusted to Our Lady all that we have and all that we are.

a prayer to Our Lady of Guadalupe; and Pope Paul VI sent a beautiful Golden Rose to the Basilica on March 25, 1966.

On January 27, 1979, Pope John Paul II visited the Basilica in Mexico City. He was the first pope to do so. His journey was a pilgrimage of faith. He knelt before the image of Our Lady, invoked her motherly assistance, and called upon her as Mother of the Americas. One and a half million people lined the streets to see him. He presented a diadem in honor of Our Lady of Guadalupe and offered Mass for 50,000 people gathered at the Basilica. The Pope urged Catholics to stress evangelization, spreading the Faith. The Pope prayed to Our Lady of Guadalupe: "O Mother, help us to be faithful stewards of the great mysteries of God, help us to teach the truth proclaimed by your Son and to spread love, which is the chief commandment and the first fruit of the Holy Spirit." He offered the Church in America to Our Lady as her own. He asked her to embrace everyone, to seek everyone out with motherly care. He asked her as Queen of Peace to save the nations and people of America from war, hatred, and subversion. He called upon her as Mother of Mercy, the Mother of the Americas. He prayed to her for all the Bishops that they might lead the faithful along the paths of an intense Christian life. He entrusted to her all that we have and all that we are. He entrusted vocations to her and asked her as "Mother of Fair Love" to protect our families. The Holy Father prayed that Holy Mary of Guadalupe would grant peace, justice, and prosperity to our people.

On May 6, 1990, on the occasion of the Holy Father's second visit to the Basilica in Mexico City, he again called upon Mary as the "Star of Evangelization." He came again to invoke her maternal help and protection on his pontifical ministry and to repeat to her with increased force:

On May 6, 1990, on the occasion of the Pope's second visit to the Basilica, he directed an appeal to the Church on the American continent to undertake a New Evangelization.

"totus tuus sum ego": I am yours entirely. The Holy Father directed an appeal to the Church on the American continent to undertake a New Evangelization. The Pope referred to the blessed soil of Mexico as being where Our Lady of Guadalupe established her throne as the Queen of the Americas. On May 7, in Veracruz, the Pope referred to Mary as the first woman to receive the Gospel message in order to announce it to others.

On May 12, 1992, the Holy Father celebrated Mass in the lower level of St. Peter's Basilica, where he dedicated a chapel in honor of Our Lady of Guadalupe. He spoke of this new chapel "taking us in spirit to the Upper Room in Jerusalem where the Apostles" devoted themselves with one accord to prayer, together with some women, and Mary the Mother of Jesus. (Acts 1:14). The Pope said: "that in Mary we will surely find the strength necessary for undertaking the new evangelization to which we are called." [7]

How can we respond to such a loving Mother's call? All mankind, particularly people in Canada, the United States, Mexico, Central and South America would do well to call upon her as Holy Mary of Guadalupe and to recognize her as Mother and Queen of America. We should follow the example of the Holy Father and entrust our entire being to her. We can commend the Church, our nations and families to her Immaculate Heart. We can put her picture in a place of honor in our homes and churches. We can pray the Rosary before her image; by doing so we offer her a precious bouquet of "roses." We can bring her into all of our problems and those of others.

The following words constitute John Paul II's dedicatory prayer to the Virgin of Guadalupe:

On May 12, 1992, the Holy Father celebrated Mass in the lower level of St. Peter's Basilica, where he dedicated a chapel in honor of Our Lady of Guadalupe.

O Immaculate Virgin, Mother of the true God and Mother of the Church! You, who from this place reveal your clemency and your pity to all those who ask for your protection, hear the prayer that we address to you with filial trust, and present it to your Son Jesus, our sole Redeemer. Mother of Mercy, Teacher of hidden and silent sacrifice, to you, who come to meet us sinners, we dedicate on this day all our being and all our love. We also dedicate to you our life, our work, our joys, our infirmities and our sorrows. Grant peace, justice, and prosperity to our peoples; for we entrust to your care all that we have and all that we are, our Lady and Mother. We wish to be entirely yours and to walk with you along the way of complete faithfulness to Jesus Christ in His Church; hold us always with your loving hand. Virgin of Guadalupe, Mother of the Americas, we pray to you for all the Bishops, that they may lead the faithful along paths of intense Christian life, of love, and humble service of God and souls. Contemplate this immense harvest, and intercede with the Lord that He may instill a hunger for holiness in the whole People of God, and grant abundant vocations of priests and religious, strong in the faith and zealous dispensers of God's mysteries. Grant to our homes the grace of loving and respecting life in its beginnings, with the same love with which you conceived in your womb the life of the Son of God. Blessed Virgin Mary, Mother of Fair Love, protect our families, so that they may always be united, and bless the upbringing of our children. Our hope, look upon us with compassion, teach us to go continually to Jesus and, if we fall, help us to rise again, to return to Him, by means of the confession of our faults and sins in the Sacrament of Penance, which gives peace to the soul. We beg you to grant us a great love for all the holy Sacraments, which are, as it were, the signs that your Son left us on earth. Thus, Most Holy Mother, with the peace of God in our conscience, with out hearts free from evil and hatred, we will be able to bring to all, true joy and true peace, which come to us from your Son, our Lord Jesus Christ, who with God the Father and the Holy Spirit, lives and reigns for ever and ever. Amen.

7
River of Light and Health of the Sick

THE STORY OF Our Lady's apparitions to Juan Diego is well known. What is not so well known is that Mary made a separate visit to Juan Diego's ailing uncle, Juan Bernardino, on December 12, 1531, in Tolpetlac, nine miles from Tepeyac Hill. Juan Bernardino was instantly and miraculously cured of the typhus which threatened his life. Our Lady requested that Juan Bernardino inform the Bishop of Mexico City, Bishop Zumarraga, of the cure. It was not to Juan Diego, but to Juan Bernardino that Mary made known her wish to be invoked under the title of Holy Mary of Guadalupe.

In 1911, almost 400 years after the apparitions, a church was built on the site of Juan Bernardino's home, where the miraculous cure had taken place. Pope Pius XII has granted indulgences to people who visit this shrine on the 12th of each month. This shrine was for a time in a state of neglect; a commission was formed and the shrine was restored and made into a parish. The villagers built a house for a priest and a seminary was established. Tolpetlac has since been a "garden of vocations."

In the church, above the tabernacle, there is a painting by Luis Toral depicting the miraculous cure of Juan

Bernardino by our Lady. In 1979 Bishop Don Magin Torreblanco of Texcoco, the diocese in which Tolpetlac is located, asked the Holy Father, John Paul II, for permission to crown this image of Our Lady. The Bishop wished to honor her as "Health of the Sick." On January 27, 1979, the day of the Pope's historic visit to the Basilica in Mexico City, the Pope gave written permission for the coronation.

On December 16, 1979, Cardinal Ernesto Corripio Ahumada and Bishop Torreblanco crowned the image of Our Lady of Guadalupe in Tolpetlac as "Health of the Sick." While the Cardinal was giving his inspiring homily during the Mass, there appeared a surprisingly intense ray of light from above, illumining Mary's hands and lap. At that very moment the Cardinal was making clear the truth of the Gospel using figures of speech such as the following:

> Mary is like a river always flowing — she is always sending light inspiring love; The endless source of that love and guidance is Jesus Christ; let's hope that river of light, love and hope reaches every man so that the whole world knows that love; she has brought us that light and love not only for us individually but also to unite us and to make us feel that we all belong to the same kingdom and that we must enlarge it and pass it on everywhere, carrying the teaching of Christ to all our brothers. In that way we will carry Mary with us and people will see Mary through us. Mary's hands extend to us like a stream of light that makes darkness disappear. Her love makes the darkness of doubt and fear disappear.

The actual ray of light which appeared as the Cardinal was uttering these words seems to have been a special gift of God. As the Cardinal and Bishop approached the picture in order to crown the image, the ray became more intense — seeming to indicate God's approval and satisfaction. The crown was made by Victor Boniela, but the idea for its design was Father Salvador Sollano's. The

On December 16, 1979, Cardinal Corripio Ahumada and Bishop Torreblanco crowned the image of Our Lady of Guadalupe as "Health of the Sick," with the crown which was the gift of Pope John Paul II. This took place at Tolpetlac, nine miles from Mexico City.

crown is in gold and silver; the base is a Rosary and the top is a cross.

The villagers of Tolpetlac had prayed and sung to the angels for three days. They had invited the angels to come and join in the crowning of Mary, our Mother and Queen. It was a call to the Heavenly Militia, made to insure that both heaven and earth could unite in the crowning of Our Lady of Guadalupe as the "Health of the Sick."

The ray of light was a sign of God's pleasure in the crowning of His Blessed Mother, precisely at this place, where she gave herself the name of "Guadalupe," which means "a river of light." It seems to be visible proof that God wants to keep communicating His light and love to mankind through Mary in this place of her visit to Juan Bernardino. It is a sign that Mary will keep communicating the light that comes from Christ to all the sick. Many, like Juan Diego and Juan Bernardino, will be converted by her love. We should pray that all people in Canada, the United States, Mexico, Central America, and South America will invoke Holy Mary of Guadalupe as the Mother and Queen of America and as the "Health of the Sick." She is indeed the merciful mother of all who invoke her help and place their trust in her.

Let us recognize and proclaim Our Lady of Guadalupe as a River of Light and Love so as to be open to the Light Who is Christ. It is worthy of note that the Rosary is at the base of the crown of Our Lady of Guadalupe. The Rosary is itself a crown of roses offered to Mary, a symbol of the coronation which her children continually offer her. The Holy Father, John Paul II, has let it be known that his favorite prayer is the Rosary and has asked us to pray the Rosary for him who gave his permission for the crowning of "Mary, Health of the Sick" and who declares that the time has come for devotion and piety to Holy Mary of Guadalupe to grow.

8

The Rosary Message of Guadalupe

T HE DOMINICANS were sent to Mexico in 1526 at the command of Spain's Charles V. The first group of 12 were welcomed by the Franciscans "with no less charity than joy." In fact, the Dominicans remained with them for three months until their own convent was ready.

The Dominican Father Domingo de Betanzos immediately opened a novitiate in Mexico City. His zeal and sanctity were such that crowds of young Castilians who had left Spain in search of riches and adventure gave up their dreams of worldly glory in order to receive the holy habit from him. Under the direction of another Dominican, Father Gonzales, the Dominican novitiate in Mexico prospered and in fewer than three years a large group of men had been prepared for the service of God. Thus, in 1530, the year before the apparitions of Our Lady of Guadalupe, the expansion of the Dominican order in Mexico was about to begin. Although up to this time the early Franciscan missionaries had worked fervently to convert the Indians, they had disappointing results. A handful of friars struggling with a foreign language and scattered among the multitudes in such a vast territory seemed woefully inadequate to their task.

When he was assigned to Oaxaca, Father Gonzales faced a similar situation. He found the Indians no more agreeable than the Franciscans had found them. However, Father Gonzales was inspired to preach the Holy Rosary to the Indians in a new way. He decided to appeal to their artistic sense. He had the mysteries of the Rosary printed on canvas, which was easy to handle, and he displayed the canvas when talking about these mysteries. This method met with great success. Filled with wonder, the Indians came in great numbers to this Dominican priest and brought him their little children to be baptized. In this way the first Rosary Crusade among the Indians in Mexico preceded the apparitions of Holy Mary of Guadalupe.

In Mary's appearances on Tepeyac Hill she seems to invite everyone to contemplate all that occurred when she sent Juan Diego with the express command "to repeat all that you have seen and admired and to omit nothing in the telling." Perhaps her words and actions also conceal hidden mysteries under the symbolism of the roses. If this is the case, we would do well to study each detail with loving admiration for our own instruction. Might not her appearance on Tepeyac Hill suggest a Rosary message which has thus far escaped observation?

From the variety of flowers that Juan found on the top of the hill, he was told to pick only *Castilian roses*. After taking the *roses in her own hands, and rearranging them*, and placing them in his cloak, Mary definitely asserts that "this cluster of roses is the sign which you are to take to the Bishop. [8] This seems to be a figure of the Rosary devotion which Mary entrusted to St. Dominic, the saint of the province of Castile in Spain, to use in his preaching and conversion of souls. This interpretation is supported when we consider the background of St. Dominic's method of inculcating doctrines concerning Mary—his use of

The Rosary and the image of Mary are two wonderful gifts from God. Through our Rosaries we offer Our Lady of Guadalupe beautiful roses and pray that she will imprint her virtues on the tilma of our souls.

images taken from Christ's life and from meditations of the mysteries of the Rosary. "What is the Rosary but a huge cluster of mystic roses—Our Fathers and Hail Marys—arranged into the mysteries of the Incarnation, Redemption, and Eternal Life and preached by St. Dominic and his followers down through the centuries? [9] "Superimpose the teachings of the Rosary on the sackcloth of penance, permeated by contemplative prayer, and the character of Mary will emerge, even in unlikely souls. Watered by the dew of divine grace, they will begin to reproduce celestial tints of many kinds of virtues, sprinkled throughout with the gold of divine charity. [10]

The miraculous image of Guadalupe is a pictorial expression of the way that the Rosary operates in souls. Devotion to the Holy Rosary and to Holy Mary of Guadalupe are among the special ways by which souls can direct themselves to the Blessed Virgin and pay the the honor which they owe her. Europe's prayers of the Rosary, begging for Mary's intercession, helped to win the victory over the Turks in the battle of Lepanto in 1571, and Admiral Andrea Doria's supplication before his copy of the miraculous image of Guadalupe helped the Christians during the worst part of the battle. In the same way that Mary converted the rough, coarse cloth of Juan Diego's cloak into a texture much more like fine silk, Mary can also change our poor human nature through the softening influence of divine grace which comes with a constant devout meditation on the mysteries of the Rosary.

Just as Mary's mystic roses on Tepeyac Hill flourished into her miraculous image on Juan Diego's cloak, so too we can beseech her to transform our souls through the contemplation of the mysteries of the Rosary. Moreover, we can ask that she imprint on our souls her likeness, not physically but spiritually so we will be better able to imitate her sanctity. Although this seems too miraculous a transformation even to hope for, the image of Our Lady of Guadalupe should remind us that Mary through Christ's powers can transform anything—whether it be something so simple as a cloak or so complex as a soul. Just as Bishop Zumarraga believed in the possibility of the cloak's being transformed into a holy image when he saw Mary's Castilian roses, so too we, when we behold Our Lady of Guadalupe, should believe in prayer's fundamental power to transform in the most miraculous fashion. It may also hearten us to remember the testimony of many popes to the efficacy of prayer and particularly to the sanctifying power of praying the Rosary. Being the "faithful Spouse of the Holy Spirit," Mary can teach her children through her own example. With His delicate divine prodding, the Holy Spirit will create a masterpiece in each prayerful soul—radiating beauty like that on the cloak which depicts Holy Mary of Guadalupe.

As Americans, as simple lovers of the Rosary, we should try to cultivate great devotion to Holy Mary of Guadalupe seeing in her image visible representation of what our inner spiritual lives might become when directed by the grace that comes from praying the Rosary. This will be especially true if we respond faithfully to Mary's direction when we meditate on the mysteries of the Rosary. We have the testimony of the sovereign pontiffs who affirm the sanctifying power of the Rosary, especially John Paul II. He believes that "the Rosary, recited slowly and meditated upon, personally, in the family, in community will gradually let you enter the sentiments of Christ and Mary, recalling all the events which are the key of our salvation." He believes that "with Mary, you will open your soul to the Holy Spirit, so that He may inspire all the great tasks that await you." John Paul II truly believes that the Rosary, along with the Angelus, should be for every Christian, a kind of "spiritual oasis" in the course of the day, to help them attain courage and confidence.

* * *

If you wish to belong to a Rosary family, one started by St. Dominic under the inspiration of Mary, you can register your name with the Confraternity of the Holy Rosary. This is a spiritual association whose members have the obligation, which does not bind under sin, of reciting the 15 mysteries of the Rosary, while devoutly meditating on them, during the course of each week. "For wherever a person fulfills his obligation of reciting the Rosary according to the rule of the confraternity, he includes in his intentions all its members, and they in turn render him service many times over. (Ubi primuni, Leo XIII, October 2, 1898.) Members receive many indulgences by the Holy See—participation in all Masses, prayers, and good works of the Dominicans and the special protection of Mary. Members also receive the benefit of all co-members' prayers and good works. St. John Vianney said, "If anyone has the happiness of being in the Confraternity of the Holy Rosary, he and she have in all corners of the globe brothers and sisters who pray for them." Ecclesiastical writers have called the confraternity "the praying army enrolled by St. Dominic under the banner of the Mother of God." If you wish to be a member, send your complete name and address to:

Rosary Center
Dominican Fathers
P.O. Box 3617
Portland, OR 97208

9

Miracles and Modern Studies

OF COURSE, there are many miraculous occurrences attributed to Our Lady of Guadalupe. On December 12, Mary cured Juan Bernardino who was dying in the town of Tolpetlac — and on December 26, the day that the image was being transferred to the new adobe hermitage, she performed another miracle. A Chickimeca Indian was accidently struck by an arrow which killed him. When they took him to the feet of the Virgin's picture, asking her intercession with great confidence and devotion, Mary revived him and, miraculously, he showed no sign of a wound or scar.

Throughout the following years, equally remarkable miracles occurred. In 1629, Mexico City experienced its worst flood. The entire city was flooded and 30,000 Indians died. The Archbishop decided to remove the image from the church and bring it to the Cathedral in an effort to end the flood through Mary's intercession. The city was saved and rebuilt and Our Lady of Guadalupe was acclaimed as the deliverer of the city. In August 1736, an unknown fever spread throughout the nation. Thousands of Indians died in a very short time. The citizens decided to proclaim Our Lady of Guadalupe, the Patroness of the Capital. Historians agree that the plague was over as soon as the patronage was decreed. On November 14, 1921, a bomb, hidden in a bouquet of flowers, was put on the altar with the intention of destroying the image; the bomb did explode, causing much damage, but nothing happened to the precious image or to the glass which covers it. In the Basilica, on every available wall, there are signs and symbols of favors received; they number into the thousands.

The new Basilica was dedicated on October 12, 1976. The sacred image was transferred with much solemnity on that day from the old Basilica to the new. The new Basilica is the fourth home of Holy Mary of Guadalupe. It stands on level ground near the base of Tepeyac Hill. It is located about four miles north of the center of old Mexico City, which is known as the Zocalo.

In recent years, some of the scientific discoveries concerning the image of Our Lady of Guadalupe have been almost as interesting as some of the miraculous events connected with it. On May 7, 1979, 40 frames of infra-red photographs were taken of the miraculous image. The methods of study were similar to those used by American specialists studying the Shroud of Turin since 1978. The infra-red photos were taken by Dr. Philip C. Callahan, a research biophysicist at the University of Florida and the United States Department of Agriculture. Dr. Callahan, along with Professor Jody Smith of Pensacola State Junior College and other specialists, concluded that the original miraculous image is unexplainable as a human work, but they found that there have been additions made by painters. In the words of the researchers themselves:

> The original image on the tilma [cloak] has qualities of color and uses the weave of the cloth itself in a way no human painter and no substance known in painting can effect. . . . The infra-red

The new Basilica was dedicated on October 12, 1976. The sacred image was transferred with much solemnity on that day from the old Basilica to the new one.

study shows that there are no guidelines under the original image, such as an artist might use. Mary stands in simplicity on a black rock. She wears a plain rose-colored garment, and an unadorned blue-green mantle. There may or may not have been an original sunburst around Our Lady. The gold rays now visible have been put on the tilma and are metallic, and do not allow penetration by infra-red photography. The study also concludes that the tilma was not sized as is usual with cloth before it is painted on, nor does it have a protective coat of varnish.[11]

Dr. Callahan says, "In conclusion, the original holy image is inexplicable but the tassel and moon were probably added in the sixteenth century by an Indian, and the Gothic decoration and background sunburst were also added by human hands, probably in the seventeenth century, in order to cover water damage and to preserve outer fabric."[12]

As Father Christopher Rengers, O.F.M. Cap., points out:

Other human additions are decorative and symbolic. They are the angel, the clouds and sky beyond the sunburst, 'the Aztec fold' at the feet, the fur cuffs at the neck and wrists, the black cross brooch, the mantle's gold stars and trim and the thin-line tracery on the rose-colored garment. The black edging for the garments and hands is an addition, and the fingers have been shortened. A crown, still dimly visible, has been painted in and painted out.[13]

In his final conclusion Dr. Callahan relates why the original image of Our Lady of Guadalupe on Juan Diego's tilma cannot be explained as the work of human hands:

The original figure including the rose robe, blue mantle, hands and face is inexplicable. In terms of this infra-red study there is no way to explain either the kind of color pigments utilized, nor the maintenance of color luminosity and brightness of pigments over the centuries. Furthermore, when consideration is given to the fact that there is no underdrawing, sizing, or varnish, and that the weave of the fabric itself is utilized to give the portrait depth, no explanation of the portrait is possible by infra-red techniques. It is remarkable that in over four centuries there is no fading or cracking of the original figure on any portion of the agave tilma, which being unsized should have deteriorated centuries ago.[14]

Dr. Callahan believes that many of the human additions were made after the image itself was damaged by water in the flood of 1629. As Father Rengers mentions, Dr. Callahan, who is also a painter, considers "the additions an enhancement of the original." As Callahan says himself, "Any single addition, whether the moon, 'Aztec fold', gold and black border, angel or whatever, does not alone enhance the portrait. Taken together, however, the effect is overwhelming. . . . It is as if God and man had worked jointly to create a masterpiece."[15]

On May 7, 1979, some 40 frames of infra-red photographs were taken of the miraculous image by Dr. Philip C. Callahan.

10

The 450th Anniversary

D ECEMBER 12, 1981, was the 450th anniversary of the apparitions of Our Lady of Guadalupe to Juan Diego. On the anniversary, the Holy Father celebrated Mass in St. Peter's Basilica. In his homily he said: "There are a great many hearts which, from all the nations of America, from north to south, converge in devout pilgrimage towards the Mother of Guadalupe."[16] The Holy Father talked about the message of Guadalupe and pointed to Mary's virginal motherhood and her being implored as the "ever-perfect Virgin."

He also talked about the aspect, proclaimed in the Guadalupe message, of Mary's spiritual motherhood of all men, which is closely united with her divine motherhood. The Pope then referred to the teachings of the Second Vatican Council: "She conceived, brought forth, and nourished Christ, she presented Him to the Father in the temple, shared her Son's sufferings as He died on the cross. Thus, in a wholly singular way she cooperated by her obedience, faith, hope and burning charity in the work of the Savior in restoring supernatural life to souls. For this reason she is a mother to us in the order of grace."[17] (Lumen Gentium, 61)

The Holy Father expressed that he would have been happy to be present there among the people at the Basilica

On December 12, 1981, Cardinal Casaroli, Secretary of
State, was the Papal Legate for the 450th anniversary of
Holy Mary of Guadalupe's apparitions.

in Mexico City for this great occasion; however, since this was impossible, he was sending the Secretary of State, Cardinal Casaroli, to represent him during the celebrations. The Holy Father addressed Cardinal Casaroli before leaving Rome for Mexico City with these words: "It only remains for you who have been given this opportunity and share our thoughts and know our mind, to repeat and carefully explain all that we said there three years ago."[18] The Holy Father hoped that the ceremonies commemorating the origins of the devotion to Our Lady of Guadalupe, would become the source and cause of a more lively devotion to Mary. The Pope said: "In this way, the sanctuary may become a sort of center from which one may seek a model of Christian simplicity and of familiar converse with God: from which derives an abundance of divine graces and consolations; from which the relations between pastors and faithful, and between all followers of Christ are strengthened; finally from which the light of the Gospel of Christ will shine out over the whole world by means of the miraculous image of His Mother."[19]

The Holy Father talked about Mary leading us to Christ. He said: "This cultural reality in which the presence of Our Lady and Mother is so deeply felt, is a potential element which must be turned to advantage with all its evangelizing promise for the future, in order to lead the faithful people by Mary's hand, to Christ, the center of Christian life."[20] The Pope prayed to Mary in these words: "And since you are the Empress of the Americas, protect all the nations of the American continent and the ones that brought faith and love for you there."[21]

Cardinal Casaroli, the Papal Legate, in his homily at the Basilica of Our Lady of Guadalupe on December 12, 1981, told the beautiful story of Mary's visits to Juan Diego and her sweet words to him on Tepeyac Hill. The

Cardinal's words were: "And from that humble height the Virgin's eye turned to the immense expanses of the Americas, from the impassable peaks to the deep valleys, from the windswept plateaus to the boundless plains, as far as the extreme end of the continent, where the two oceans that surround it unite in a stormy embrace. It was as if the Mother's gentle smile illuminated them all with love and hope. Just as the sun, reflecting its brightness in the rivers and lakes, bring forth, as it were, new suns, so the Virgin's smile, beaming from Tepayac Hill, seemed to be reflected in every part of this continent."[22] The Cardinal referred to the sanctuary of Our Lady of Guadalupe as the Marian heart of the Americas. He prayed to her: "O our merciful Mother! From this house of yours and from all your sanctuaries scattered all over the Americas and throughout the world, lend your ears and your help to those who invoke you. O Mother of God and our Mother: give us peace! Amen."[23]

In the course of the celebrations at Mexico City for the 450th anniversary of the apparitions, a monument dedicated to the Holy Father was inaugurated. During the ceremony, Cardinal Casaroli said: "Today we inaugurate this monument, which will perpetuate in your midst, in the Marian center of Mexico and of the Americas, his mild and beloved fatherly figure: Perhaps you do not need this, you who have carved his effigy in your hearts; but the monument is addressed to the future generations which will come here, so that they will remember that Pope John Paul II came here one day, a pilgrim like them, to lay his supplications and his hopes at the feet of Our Lady of Guadalupe."[24]

* * *

In the course of the celebrations of the 450th anniversary, a monument dedicated to the Holy Father was inaugurated — addressed to future generations so they will remember that Pope John Paul II came here one day, a pilgrim like them.

Here in the United States there are those who also wish to lay their supplications and hopes at the feet of Our Lady of Guadalupe. And to help accomplish this, there was established a National Shrine-Center in Allentown, Pennsylvania.

On March 19, 1974, a committee in St. Louis, with Bishop Sidney Metsger of El Paso present as honorary chairman, chose the Immaculate Conception Church in Allentown as the site for a National Shrine-Center for the Patroness of the Americas. This church was founded by St. John Neumann in 1857. This was done after consultation by mail with all U.S. Ordinaries. All were quickly notified of the decision. The then-Bishop of Allentown, Joseph McShea, welcomed the Mother of the Americas Apostolate in his diocese. The present Bishop of Allentown is Most Reverend Thomas J. Welsh.

11

Star of Evangelization

IN 1992, WE IN THE AMERICAS, entered the final stages of a nine year novena which Pope John Paul II inaugurated in 1984 in order to prepare for the 500th Anniversary of the Evangelization of the Americas. On October 12, 1984, in Santo Domingo, the Dominican Republic, the Pope inaugurated this novena of years by presenting each Bishops' conference from North, Central, and South America, a large wooden cross, similar to the first one planted on the shores of Santo Domingo, the Cradle of Catholicism in the New World. Santo Domingo was the first diocese of the Americas and site of the first Mass celebrated in the Americas in 1494.

In 1979, John Paul II visited Santo Domingo for the first time. In his homily at the outdoor Mass before 250,000 people, he said, "Evangelization constitutes the way and the vocation of the Church, her most profound identity. She exists to evangelize." In 1990, on May 7, in Veracruz, Mexico, the Pope talked about Faith and the New Evangelization. He said "To evangelize means to announce the Good News. And the Good News which the Christian communicates to the world is that God, who alone is Lord, is merciful to all his creatures, loves man with limitless love and has sought to intervene personally in his history

The 16th century Cathedral of Santo Domingo, the oldest in America, was the scene of the Holy Father's Mass with priests and religious on October 10, 1992, for the celebration of the fifth centenary of evangelization in America.

by means of his Son Jesus Christ, who died and rose for us, to free us from sin and from all its consequences and to make us sharers in his divine life."[25]

The purpose of the celebration of the Fifth Centenary is to spark a new strategy for evangelization in the Americas. In the words of John Paul II, the Quincentenary should be the dawn of a new evangelization: new in its ardor, its methods, its expression." Quoting Vatican II, the Pope describes "missionary activity" as the greatest and holiest duty of the Church" (Redemptoris Missio, 63). The Pope calls the 1990's the decade of evangelization.

The Pope is encouraging everyone in the Americas to participate in the "New Evangelization," and has asked in prayer, for Our Lady of Guadalupe to be the "Star of Evangelization."

On October 9-14, 1992, the Holy Father visited Santo Domingo to honor the 500th Anniversary of the Evangelization of the Americas. During this time, he attended the Fourth General Conference of the Latin American Bishops. The conference's theme was "The new evangelization, human development, Christian culture: 'Jesus Christ, the same yesterday, today, and forever.'"

On October 9th, upon his arrival in Santo Domingo, the Pope mentioned that "on this apostolic visit, he had come to celebrate, first and foremost, Jesus Christ, the first and greatest Evangelist, who entrusted his Church with the task of proclaiming his message of salvation throughout the world. [26]At the Mass on October 11, the Pope spoke of the wonderful array of saints and blessed who adorn almost the whole of America's geography. He spoke of their lives being the mature fruits of evangelization and the model and source of inspiration for the new evangelists. At the end of the Mass, the Pope spoke of the arrival of Christ's Gospel in the Americas and how it bore the

On October 12, 1992, at the Marian shrine of Our Lady of Altagracia in the Dominican Republic, the Pope, before this image of Mary, consecrated to Mary the present and past of the Americas.

stamp of Mary. He mentioned how her name and image figured prominently on Columbus' ship, the Santa Maria, and how his crew invoked her by singing the Salve Regina. He spoke of Mary's particular love for each nation and people of America. On October 12, the Pope celebrated Mass at the Marian shrine of Our Lady of Altagracia in the city of Higuey. It is the oldest Marian shrine in America. During the Mass, the Holy Father spoke of Mary as being a model for today's believers and that she must be the Star of the new evangelization. He spoke of Mary as being the Gospel transformed into life and as being the highest and most perfect fulfillment of the Christian message.

During the Mass at the shrine, the Holy Father recited the following Act of Entrustment, consecrating to Mary, the present and past of the Americas:

1. *Hail Mary, full of grace: I greet you*, O Virgin Mary, in the words of the angel.

I bow before your image, patroness of the Dominican Republic, to proclaim your blessed title of Altagracia.

You were "full of grace," filled by the love of the Most High, made fruitful by the power of the Spirit, to be the Mother of Jesus, the Son born from on high.

I contemplate you, Virgin of Altagracia, in the mystery revealed by your image: the birth of your Son, the incarnate Word, who chose to dwell among us, whom you adore and show to us so that he may be recognized as the Saviour of the world.

You go before us in the work of the new evangelization which is and must always be the proclamation and confession of Christ, "the Way, the Truth and the Life."

2. *Holy Mary, Mother of God:*

On this day, 12 October 1992, before your image I recall the completion of five hundred years since the Gospel of Christ came to the peoples of America on a ship which bore your name and image: the "Santa Maria."

With the whole Church in America I intone the "Magnificat" because, through your motherly love, God came to visit his people in the sons and daughters who inhabited these lands in order to make his dwelling among them, to communicate to them the fullness of salvation in Christ and join them in a single Spirit to the holy Catholic Church.

You are the Mother of America's first evangelization and the precious gift which Christ gave us through the proclamation of the message of salvation.

3. *Queen and Mother of America:*
With the pastors and faithful of this Continent, I venerate you in all the shrines and images which bear your name, in the cathedrals, parishes and chapels, in the cities and villages, along the oceans, river and lakes, in the forests and on mountain heights.
I invoke you in the languages of all its inhabitants, and I express to you the filial love of all their hearts.
For five hundred years you have been present in every part of these blessed lands of yours, for to say "America" is to say "Mary."
You are the loving, caring Mother of all our sons and daughters who acclaim you as "our life, our sweetness and our hope."

4. *Mother of Christ and of the Church:*
As Pastor of the universal Church, I offer and consecrate to you all your sons and daughters of America: the Bishops, priests, deacons and catechists; men and women religious; those who live their consecration in the contemplative life, or bear witness in the midst of the world.
I entrust to you the children and young people, the elderly, the poor and sick, each of the local Churches, all the families and Christian communities.
I offer you their joys and hopes, their fears and anguish, their prayers and efforts for a kingdom of justice and peace, enlightened by the Gospel of truth and life.
You, whose place is so close to both God and mankind, through your motherly mediation, present to your Son Jesus Christ the offering of the priestly people of the Americas; ask his pardon for the injustices committed, and accompany our thanksgiving with your canticle of praise.

5. *Virgin of Hope and Star of Evangelization:*
I ask you to preserve and increase the gift of faith and Christian life which the peoples of America received five centuries ago.

Intercede with your Son, that this Continent may be a land of peace and hope where love conquers hatred, unity overcomes rivalry, generosity defeats selfishness, the truth wins out over falsehood, justice vanquishes iniquity, and peace dominates over violence.

May there always be respect for the life and dignity of every human person, the identity of ethnic minorities, the legitimate rights of the indigenous peoples, the genuine values of the family and of the autochthonous cultures.

O Star of Evangelization, make everyone zealous for the proclamation of the Good News so that Jesus Christ may always be known, loved and served, the blessed fruit of your womb, the Revelation of the Father and the One who bears the Spirit, "the same yesterday, today and forever." Amen.

As the third millennium draws near, one can sense that God is preparing a great springtime for Christianity, as John Paul II has maintained. Mary is playing a very important part in this new springtime. At the first Pentecost, when the Apostles prayed with Mary in the Upper Room, God had Mary watching over, with her prayer, the beginning of the evangelization prompted by the Holy Spirit. Now, the Church is once again gathered together with Mary preparing for a new Pentecost.

After his return to Rome from Santo Domingo, the Holy Father said this of Santo Domingo and the new evangelization: "May Santo Domingo be a new Upper Room, where the sucessors of the Apostles, gathered in prayer with the Mother of Christ, prepare the way for the new evangelization of all America. On the threshold of the third millennium, may the pastors know how to offer the world "Christ, who is the same yesterday, today and forever." [27]

On December 7, 1992, in a special ceremony, the Holy Father presented the new *Catechism of the Catholic Church* to the world. The Pope said: "The publication of the text must certainly be counted among the major events of the

Pope John Paul II officially presented the new Catechism of the Catholic Church in a special ceremony on December 7, 1992.

Church's recent history. It is a precious gift because it faithfully reiterates the Christian Doctrine of all times." [28] During the ceremony, he spoke of Mary: "May the Blessed Virgin, whose Immaculate Conception we celebrate tomorrow, help us to accept and appreciate this precious gift and be a model and support for us in giving others the divine Word which the *Catechism of the Catholic Church* presents to the faithful and to the whole world." [29]

On December 8, the Solemnity of the Immaculate Conception, the Holy Father celebrated Mass in Rome's St. Mary Major Basilica. During the homily, the Pope said: "Together with the Mother of God, the Church today offers thanks for the gift of the Council which was opened on October 11 thirty years ago, precisely on the feast of Mary's maternity. The community of believers today offers thanks for the post-conciliar catechism which is a compendium of the truth proclaimed by the Church throughout the world. This compendium of the Catholic faith, requested by the Bishops gathered in the Extraordinary Assembly of the Synod in 1985, is the most mature and complete fruit of the council's teaching and presents it in the rich framework of the whole of ecclesial Tradition. Together we all place the new *Catechism of the Catholic Church*—which is, at the same time the gift of the revealed Word to humanity and the fruit of the work of Bishops and theologians—together we all place it in the hands of her who, as Mother of the Word, took into her arms the Firstborn of all creatures." [30]

The Holy Father has asked that the new catechism be used by Bishops in fulfilling their mission of proclaiming the faith and by the faithful who wish to deepen their faith. It is also directed at non-Catholics, to all Christians who wish to know the Catholic faith. The Pope said: "The *Catechism of the Catholic Church* is offered to every

On December 8, 1992, the Pope kneels at the altar of Rome's St. Mary Major Basilica where he placed the new Catechism of the Catholic Church in the hands of Mary and entrusted it to her as a valuable instrument of the new evangelization.

individual who asks us to give an account of the hope that is in us and who wants to know what the Catholic Church believes."[31] The Pope said this of the new catechism: "Through the intercession of Mary most holy, 'a living catechism and the Mother and model of catechists,' may this *Catechism of the Catholic Church* be a further, valued instrument for the renewed apostolic mission and evangelization of the universal Church on the eve of the third Christian millennium."[32]

The Pope encourages people to beseech Mary to give the whole Church a new impetus in the task of spreading the Good News of salvation, especially at this time when the Church is called to a new effort of evangelization. How fitting it is to implore Our Lady of Guadalupe for this intention, as Pope John XXIII called her the Heavenly Missionary of the New World and Mother and Teacher of the Faith to the peoples of the Americas, and Pope John Paul II calls her the Star of Evangelization. May Our Lady of Guadalupe inspire us and enlighten us to read and meditate on the *Catechism of the Catholic Church* and thus become participators in the new evangelization.

Conclusion

I T IS VERY important for us to remember that popes from the time of the apparitions have hailed Our Lady of Guadalupe as the Queen and Mother of our hemisphere. Her apparitions, her remarkable image, her wonderful cures, and her constant intercession for those in the Americas have all been affirmed, and devotion to her encouraged by the popes. The late Pope Pius XII reminded us of Mary's position as a guardian of orthodoxy and enjoined all citizens of the Americas to pray to her for fidelity.

Our Lady of Guadalupe, who appeared at the start of the evangelization process of America, is being called upon by John Paul II to be the guiding star of the new evangelization. The Rosary is a wonderful prayer for this time of evangelization. Seeing that any evangelization process has its basis in the mysteries of Christ: in His Incarnation, Redemption, and Resurrection, we come to see how fitting the Rosary is for the evangelization of ourselves and others. John Paul II said of the Rosary, "In this prayer, we unite ourselves to Mary like the Apostles gathered together in the Upper Room after Christ's Ascension." [33] How fitting it is that we unite our prayer to that of Mary—making our homes living Cenacles where we pray for an outpouring of the Holy Spirit in a continuous Pentecost for the family, the Church, and the world.

We pray to Mary that our strategies and plans for the new evangelization be in conformity with the Second

Vatican Council; also, to enlighten us in the reading and meditating on the new Catechism of the Catholic Church; and to help us develop a sound devotion to her according to the mind of the Church, especially according to Chapter 8 of the Dogmatic Constitution, Lumen Gentium, and the encyclical letter, Redemptoris Mater (Mother of the Redeemer) of John Paul II. The program for the new evangelization must be achieved as John Paul II has said: "By presenting Mary as the highest embodiment of the Christian message, as its most inspiring model to follow." [34]

So that our continents of North, Central, and South America be continents of hope, we entrust our hope to Mary, who always hoped. In Our Lady of Guadalupe, "the first one to evangelize America," we will surely find the strength necessary to be faithful to Christ and His Church, and to undertake the new evangelization to which we are being called to by Pope John Paul II.

Our Lady of Guadalupe said: "Am I not here who am your Mother? Are you not under my shadow and protection? Am I not your fountain of life? Are you not in the folds of my mantle, in the crossing of my arms?" These words by which Mary described her motherly closeness to Blessed Juan Diego and to all her spiritual children can best be explained by her spiritual son, the Vicar of Christ, John Paul II:

"Together with God, in the light of the divine glory, Mary contemplates each and every one of her children in each and every moment of their life and looks upon them at times of joy and sadness, in moments of difficulty, at times of solitude, when they fall and when they pick themselves up. There is not a single moment of our life, not even a heartbeat, in which we are not lovingly accompanied by the heart of Mary." [35]

About the Author

Robert Feeney is a native of Alexandria, Virginia. He holds a Master of Science degree in Physical Education from the University of Dayton and has taught physical education on the university, high school and grade school level. His Marian apostolate includes five years working at the Basilica of the National Shrine of the Immaculate Conception in Washington, D.C. On April 28, 1973, the late Cardinal Patrick O'Boyle, then Archbishop of Washington and chairman of the Board of Trustees of the Shrine, presented him with a plaque reading, "Apostle of Mary" for his work. He has been giving slide lectures on Our Lady of Guadalupe throughout the U.S. since 1976. He is a member of the Third Order of St. Dominic and author of the book, *The Rosary: "The Little Summa."*

Notes

1. *Handbook on Guadalupe* (Kenosha, WI: Franciscan Marytown Press, 1974), p. 36.

2. Helen Behrens, *Virgin Mary of Guadalupe* (Mexico City: Imprenta de la Editorial Progreso, 1964), p. 18.

3. An account similar to the preceding and following can be found in almost all accounts of the apparitions of the Virgin of Guadalupe, but I have relied particularly heavily on the following sources: *Am I Not Here* by Harold Rahm, S.J. and *The Handbook on Guadalupe* which is published by the Franciscan Marytown Press in 1974.

4. Wahlig, C.J., *Juan Diego* (Mexico City: Editorial Progreso, 1971), p. 73.

5. *Ibid.* p.73.

6. *The Observer* (Monterey, CA, October 12, 1983), p. 10.

7. *L'Osservatore Romano* (Vatican City, May 20, 1992), p. 3.

8. *Rosary Message of Our Lady of Guadalupe* (Summit, NJ: Dominican Nuns, 1954), p. 18. I am indebted to this pamphlet for many ideas on the connection between the Rosary and Our Lady of Guadalupe.

9. *Ibid.*

10. *Ibid.*

11. *Immaculata* (Libertyville, IL: Franciscan Marytown Press, Dec. 81/Jan. 82), p. 13.

12. *Ibid.*, p. 14.

13. *Ibid.*

14. *Ibid.*

15. *Ibid.*

16. *L'Osservatore Romano* (Vatican City, Jan. 25, 1982), p. 11.

17. *Ibid.*

18. *Ibid.*, p. 9.

19. *Ibid.*, p. 11.

20. *Ibid.*, p. 12.

21. *Ibid.*

22. *Ibid.*

23. *Ibid.*

24. *Ibid.*
25. *L'Osservatore Romano* (Vatican City, May 14, 1990), p. 10.
26. *L'Osservatore Romano* (Vatican City, Oct. 14, 1992), p. 4.
27. *L'Osservatore Romano* (Vatican City, Oct. 28, 1992), p. 11.
28. *L'Osservatore Romano* (Vatican City, Dec. 9, 1992), p. 1.
29. Ibid., p. 2.
30. *L'Osservatore Romano* (Vatican City, Dec. 16, 1992), p. 3.
31. *L'Osservatore Romano* (Vatican City, Nov. 25, 1992), p. 3.
32. *The Pope Speaks* (Huntington, IN: Nov/Dec, 1992), p. 378.
33. *A Year With Mary* (New York, NY: Catholic Book Publishing Co., 1986), p. 227.
34. *L'Osservatore Romano* (Vatican City, Oct. 7, 1992), p. 4.
35. *L'Osservatore Romano* (Vatican City, Nov. 4, 1991).

Bibliography

Behrens, Helen. *The Virgin Mary of Guadalupe*. Mexico City: Imprenta de la Editorial Progreso, 1964.

Demarest, Donald and Coley Taylor. *The Dark Virgin: The Book on Our Lady of Guadalupe*. Freeport, ME and New York: Coley Taylor Inc./Publishers, 1956.

Handbook on Guadalupe. Kenosha, WI: Franciscan Marytown Press, 1974.

Immaculata. Libertyville, IL: Franciscan Marytown Press, Dec. 81/Jan. 82.

Lee, Rev. George, C.S.Sp. *Our Lady of Guadalupe, Patroness of the Americas*. New York: Catholic Book Publishing Co., 1947.

Leies, Herbert F., S.M. *Mother for a New World. Our Lady of Guadalupe*. Westminister, MD: Newman Press, 1964.

Our Lady of Guadalupe, The Hope of America. Lafayette, OR: Our Lady of Guadalupe Trappist Abbey, 1961.

Rahm, Harold, S.J. *Am I Not Here*. Washingon, NJ: Ave Maria Institute, 1963.

Rengers, Christopher, O.F.M. Cap. *Mary of the Americas*. New York: Alba House, 1989.

The Rosary Message of Our Lady of Guadalupe. Summit, NJ: Monastery of Our Lady of the Rosary, 1954.

Wahlig, C.J. *Juan Diego*. Mexico City, Editorial Progreso, 1971.

Watson, Simone, O.S.B. *The Cult of Our Lady of Guadalupe*. Collegeville, MN: Liturgical Press, 1964.